Let Her B

Hannah Ledyard

BookLeaf
Publishing
India | USA | UK

Presentation by *BookLeaf Publishing*

Web: www.bookleafpub.com

E-mail: info@bookleafpub.com

ISBN: 9789395969208

First edition 2023

DEDICATION

For my Boobie who is one badass bitch. She brings so much beauty to my world, to my being. I love you, Jazz.

ACKNOWLEDGEMENT

Thank you Mom and Dad for always believing in me and being my first readers. I love you both so much. Grandma, thank you for inspiring me to love stories. Jess, Tim, Jacob, Veronica, Henry, Aubrey, Dane and Stacey, you all make my heart swell. Meg and Eileen are the best second mothers anyone could ever ask for. Chris, your help with this project gave me the courage to share it with the world. Thank you, Ashley and Rosemary, for sending me notes. You inspire me every day, Jasmin. I could not have done this without you. You are the light of my life.

Bye Bye to the Burr

We dream of the icicles
That clung to the gutters of our childhoods
Hanging on with the grip of death
Never standing directly underneath the crystal
daggers
Afraid the fragile knife
Would shatter with the gentle nudge of a wistful wind
There was delight in their danger
Rejoice in the shininess of snowy season
Coldness brought warmth to the house where we
spent
A winter filled with falling flakes
Full of downhill fun
Of men made of frozen vapor rolled into three
different globes
Noses stuck out in reds and yellows
Poking out in the haze of white like the sun
Cold and happy we would sing our songs of a land
textured in evergreens
Now the cold has found a void
Where we seek and seek
And rarely find the relief
That appears with a chill
Overconsumption brought about the major melt
Greed made the ice fade away
Days lay lethargic in a heat that's here
Staying put inside our home

a Bort

The diamond
Is crushed into
The finest powder
The value not ruined
Just changed in shape
The fragments left behind
Once the price was so great
Thought never to be eclipsed
Power of particles left in the dust
Linger for those who may be lost
Dark days lay in waste for a
Future that has yet to
Arrive for the jewel
Letting go brings
The goodness
We seek

Broken Bones

The body is a temple
Healing from within
There may be pain one day
Though the hurt never remains
To haunt the frame
Because we have magic
Each and everyone

A scrape causes us to bleed
And clots without the need of a stitch
Or help from the experts
Who haunt the halls
Of a building filled with death
And broken people
Trying for some rest

Nothing is free when it comes to
Their studied care
In a country who preaches
That freedom is fair

We pay dearly when the hurt is deep
And told only a surgeon will mend
A pill can be prescribed
To drive out the scars and shakes
Sometimes the necessary treatment

Is attached to their gospel
Only healing hands
Can fix the costal erosions

More often than not
Strengths are an instinct
Buried deep inside
Rest rebuilds the bones
Nothing can break in full
When the mind is put to test
Stealth of recovery will show
When patience is practiced
You may not get up and go
But
You will find there is health

Blazing Boobies

5

She lets it all hang
Free for the world to behold
Setting eyes on fire

Buying the Bullshit

The market is filled with items for sale
An intense stench makes it hard to inhale
The treasure is covered
The truth not discovered
Wanting, buying, sold to US by a male

Bringing Baby Back

Like the rivers that flow through life
She likes to run
As free as the wind over
The once calm sea
Ripples spread out across lives of all those
touched by the bright,
Light that radiates from deep inside

Once gone
She has moved on to the next space
Only the small blocks from the calendar know
how long
She will stay put
Stay in one place for this time
A moment
And then the wings open wide

While she's away
What is left behind
Waits as silent as a
Winter night in the
Woods

Come back,
Come back
To the comfortable cradle of childhood
Letting those who fed the seed
See the marks of many
That have touched her breath

She will not stay forever
But love can
Take her home

Before getting out of Bed

I lay in bed wondering through the day
Wandering in my mind. What is to come?
Open my mouth but no words yet to say

Still in thoughts not ready to start the play
Alive though lifeless in the comfort zone
I lay in bed wondering through the day

Busy, busy with no time to delay
Wanting some waking help to pull me up
Open my mouth but no words yet to say

Time is present, only now I betray
What lies ahead in these beautiful hours
I lay in bed wondering through the day

The body moves, I will be on my way
Starting to give in to being awake
Open my mouth but still no words to say

Don't call me lazy. That is a cliché
Merely needing time to gather beliefs
I lay in bed wondering through the day
Open my mouth but no words yet to say

Baby Bear

Baby bear
Was unaware
Of the lurid affair
Between Clair
And the billionaire
The cub gave quite a scare
Lover screaming into air
We must beware
The baby bear

But baby bear
Did declare
Oh, the despair
In the questionnaire
But is the heir
Really the heir?

And even though the pair
Ask baby bear
To swear
Not to share
The cub thought it only fair
To make life square
With a bite and tear
No bit of flesh to spare

Being

I have nothing to say
Today
Maybe tomorrow the
Words will come
For someone to take in
And digest
Maybe
Figure out the problems
Of the world

I have found my baby
So the search seems to have
Died within me

There are those out there
Still trying to see
Trying to find an answer
To what will eventually be
The end of
Times
Hold the powerful
Accountable for their crimes

The heat rises
The small are left
Without a dime and clinging
To their own human soul
All they have left to their name
Theft is just another's gain
What does power truly
Cost

Life is not a game
When we all have lost

Bi

Love,
Love to everyone
Like the wagging tail
Of the happy dog
Only the straight
The narrow, the rigid
Will never know
Affection should be shared
That she is cool
Because she cares

Love the person
Not the shape
Lap it up
Before all the liquid
Has faded
Evaporated into thin
Air with the warmth
That has melted affection

Throw in the towel
On how we were raised
Now to evolve
There has to be a race
Back towards each other

An argument
Does not equate to venom
Love is all around
Floating in the air
Reach out the arms
Love will hold you near

Bad Boss

Awake before the sun to start work days
With texts abound full of excessive tasks
Wearing out one's self but still nothing pays
Control he has and wears like death's own
masks

This power proves the price of decent men
One minion, each are merely the man's drudge
Within my mind trying to stay with zen
Through peaceful thoughts I hold a gruesome
grudge

And so it is that I must state the stop
Unruly demands has placed adverse kill
Without unskilled workers business does drop
Production lays about all unfulfilled

The leader does not guide, he simply rules
So I will take with me the learn-ed tools

Balancing on Beams

A tilt to the left could take me down
Down to the cold hard ground
Right the balance
With a steady step forward
Towards the tree of life that holds the world
Attached tightly to a plank
Paved in a tight and twisting curl
Not so the path is too simple
Paved not to behave in a cruel unreasonable
manner
Follow the path
For the path
Is the path
Is my right path
And even when I put a pen to the planner
A gust of wind could tip the composure
Endure with the feet planted to my pick
Elated when I stick to the unapologetic beam
That is the route of life
Floating down stream
Not fighting to lay each brick
By stone
When the balance and the beam become one

Buzzing Baby Bumblebee

A buzzing baby bumblebee
Zooms peacefully among the greens
Searching out some violet
Some red or fuchsia or peach
Seeking to gather great amounts of feed
To bring back to the kind and quiet
Queen
Helping plant the pretty flower's seeds
Buzzing past a child's ear
Causing intense amounts of screech
In fear
But what the little human lacks
Is knowledge of the enormous need
Of that buzzing baby bumblebee

Blind Bike rides

The strap snaps in place with the sounds of
satisfaction across
The narrow face of the girl without the sense given to
most eyes
She could see in other ways that gave her endless
powers
A willingness
A grace
To conquer whatever laid in the path never before or
after to be glimpsed
She threw her legs over the steel, light as air horse
Knowing her like a twin to the touch
Movements brought to life with the strength of the
body below
Proclaiming her goodbyes
With a subtle flick of the bird-like wrist and tiny bat
to cover one iris
She was gone on the road towards an elevated
enterprise
An escape
Tasting freedom that whipped through the long dense
locks
Flying with the strength of thighs that could propel
the world in rotation
Feeling no expiration in the upward climb
Pedal
By rigorous pedal
The steed slow and steady and ready hit the peak

Striding toward the climax
Her own winded breath ringing loud to the ears
In an instant a startling honk cast out
From the insensitive horn of a beast that lazily soars
along with four wheels
Yelling to her
Wanting the small space that is a massive effort to
maintain
Feel the outrage
Fear trickles from the sightless soul making rider
release a swear
As the obnoxious driver zooms past in an agitated
huff
The crest makes a cheery conclusion
Smelling of successful sweat
The pull of gravity doing its best to give her the
wings of wonder
Wild dreams seen only in the dark
Become unrestrained with the wild glide of this
downhill ride
Arms open wide
Hugging the soothing air
She fills any void with a tranquil grasp on living here
and now
The journey almost over
And she has gotten further than the doubters could
have guessed
Even though the girl is without sight she finds she
sees best on the bike

Bagels on a Breakfast plate

We sit staring off into space
Thinking we fit the status quo
Thinking we are the onion rolls
With a simple comment
A string of neighborly complaints
The hole begins to grow
Groups break into dust all around
The solid boulder becoming brittle
Specks of sand
You are the outlier
Weirdness spilling from every pour
Standing out in blackened space
We find what was once daunting new heights
With each unique power
There is health to any sore

Bake, Burnt, Bye Bye

It is hot downstairs
Heat everywhere
Escape the madness
Relief is nowhere

I climb step by step
With a rise to the top
Flopping
With dawning exhaustion
Stops breath without air

Fever makes us loopy
With longing of summer
That spilled the sweet
Sweat from the skies

When the oven is opened
And the humans all gone
That is when
Again
Winter will come

Busy like a Bullet

I whiz through air
Little about life is fair
I move my feet
My wings
Back flies my hair

If I slow down
The pace is rare
Piercing the space
Does not calm the action
Of the human race
They cling to steal
With the call of a dare

When I'm hit
In stillness
Still not done
Tempers flair

Tough to feel
With the pace slowed to none
Can I still care?

Boiling point

The pot sits empty on cold hard burners
Waiting
Devoid of any heat

There is no time like
This time

For an overflow of passion
Face planting on hard concrete

Fill the void from the inside
Blaze switches on

Avoid watching as the inferno
Swells
Or time forgets the tick
Tock

Hold on to the moment
Of living with the calm

There is peace when
Seats give warmth to the rear

Brush with gentle strokes of anger

Too much speed
Will douse the end in fear

The faster the bubbles
Are brought
To the light of day

The tougher to keep
A lid on rage

Anger steams out with anxious moans
Causing grunts to fillet

The lid that sat atop the smooth
And quiet waters

Rubbles
Through the uncomfortable tension

Gone is the cool semblance
What is
Left are the many slaughters

Drenched in fire
Stumbling to the collect
Some quiet

What is
Right
When the fuse has blown
Too late to turn away

Tumbling to the bottom
Releasing the inside riot

Simmer the flame
Let go the fury please

Steady the shaking heart
Ease the tremble
From the kettle

Bring down the body slowly
Do not jump right into the freeze

The Bruise isn't Black, it's Blue

Ouch, the pain that hammers deep down inside
Tears stinging at this mind feel out of reach
Control over the blues and never cried
A mask, an act, taking on one of each

No visibility in all the hurt
Looking upon body and never guess
When stumbling I do not land in dirt
The skin intact and covering the stress

For so long now I crave to stick to numb
But seek the help, wanting to finally heal
As health does drive on by, out comes the thumb
Jumping aboard repair and finally feel

Of course there is the hope to mend the deep
To let out all the poison with a weep

Bleaker Blvd.

He searches for the secrets no one else can find
Knowing no one will ever hear the words
If a mystery unfolds in sight
Sitting perched atop the tower free of walls
With a face feared by the children looking towards
the gaping mouth
Months and months turn
To years and years
Of a movement that never appeared to inspire
A breach of evil spirit
Guarding with cemented enthusiasm all that lays
below
Pondering, pondering
The lives lived out on sidewalks fixed to mark each
path
Staying with the stillness
That most equate with death
The man or the monster has achieved the task
Warding off the giants that threaten to topple
Man made
Hand made structures
Looming over cities
Crowded with the junk
Too many people chuck never worried about the
landing
The silent watcher takes in all
Through unblinking vision
The cunning myth keeps the wings plastered tight

Flight will never happen
As he is stuck for eternity waiting for all our
wickedness
Visions unfolding with the viscousness of life

Birdie

Birdie birdie flaps her wings
She sits singing in a tree
Birdie birdie what does she see
Everything that we will never be
The birdie flys high
Soaring through the sky
Should she even try to land
Birdie goes on until the end
Free until the day is done
Birdie birdie flies with a song